First published in Great Britain

2023 by Jack Soley

This publication is the second edition published in 2025.

Copyright © Jack Soley, 2023

Jack Soley has asserted his moral right to be identified as the Author of this work in accordance with the Copyright Designs and Patents Act 1988.

All rights reserved. No part of this publication may be reproduced, stored in a retrieval system, or transmitted in any form or by any means, electronic, mechanical, photocopying, recording or otherwise, without the prior permission of the publisher.

A catalogue record for this book is available from the British Library.

All opinions are of that of the author and do not represent the views of the publishing company or their affiliates.

This book is published by Pomerak Ventures Ltd, registered in England & Wales under the company number 15578139.

ISBN: 9781917706049

For Eddie.

Contents

Introduction	4
Step 1: Is a name change right for me?	10
Step 2: Choosing a Name	11
Step 3: Legitimising a Document	12
Step 4: Enforcing Your Name Change	18
Changing Your Name in Scotland	34
Changing Your Name in Northern Ireland	36
Information for Foreign Citizens	38
Closing Remarks	40

Introduction

This work has come about due to a personal experience, and I decided to write this to come to the aid of others if I'm not available; this wasn't a struggle, hardship, or impossible task, but rather a challenge. My challenge was that I was born with one identity, and I wished to change it to another; you may have this challenge now, whether it be for any of these reasons:

- You have a relative who shares your surname and you no longer wish to associate with said relative.
- You're a performer who would rather go by their stage name or pseudonym full-time.
- You're getting married.
- You're getting divorced.
- You're getting adopted.
- You want to adopt a name that is more/less linked with your ethnicity.
- You're making a political statement.
- Your name is an embarrassment.

- You're going through a gender transition process.
- You're undertaking a new citizenship and wish to have a more localised name.
- You're going into hiding for legitimate purposes.

In some jurisdictions, names cannot cause offence, harm, or upset for the one using it or those who have to read it. The UK doesn't have a specific naming law, but rather a precedent after a court ruling that established a legal precedent long ago; a good example is the 1835 case of Davies v. Lowndes, Lord Chief Justice Sir Nicholas Conyngham Tindal ruled that the defendant had simply taken up and assumed the new name, the ruling found that: "a man may if he pleases, and it is not for any fraudulent purpose, take a name and work his way in the world with his new name as well as he can." ('Davies v. Lowndes' (1835) Court of Common Pleas, 1 Bing (NC) 597. (URL: https://vlex.co.uk/vid/davies-and-another-v-804578409, Accessed on 14th January 2023))

In essence, this ruling allows anyone to voluntarily relinquish their name and have a new name at any time, provided it's not for any fraudulent reason.

The process of changing your name in the UK is easy, cheap, and relatively straightforward; the complexity can be blamed on companies and people who say the process is difficult, and expensive to perform. It isn't. Anyone in England & Wales can change their name for free and without difficulty, the rules are slightly different in Scotland & Northern Ireland and I shall elaborate on their rules later.

It's worth pointing out that there are differences between changing your name as an adult and having a name at birth, specifically when the birth is registered. Names that have false titles, numbers, symbols, unpronounceable names, or names that are impractical or offensive will be likely to be rejected by the registrar in charge of registering the birth, the 17388/11 UK freedom of information request in 2011 revealed that no names were refused for birth registration during 2010; and the freedom of information request FOIR10257 filed to the DVLA by yours truly, stated that 322,857 driving licence applications were processed in 2022 which included a change of name, whether this was marriage, or a name change in its own right, is unknown and can only be open to speculation.

I've been through this process 3 times in my life, I was born with one name, I changed my name in 2015 for a joke and only changed it on my college record, bank, and bus pass; so, when I changed it back a few months later back to my original name, it wasn't as big of a challenge as was made out to be. The third and most recent change to my identity was in 2018 when I changed my middle name and surname to distance myself from a certain member of my family, the surname was changed to another surname used in the family, and the middle name was changed; partly because I didn't like my original middle name, and partly because I didn't want to snub my family by removing their last name, so my grandfather's first name, a man who I would give my utmost loyalty, became my new middle name. I could have just added their name in addition to my then-current middle name but I didn't like it and the process of changing wouldn't have been any more or less complex so I didn't forfeit any extra time, effort, and money during the process.

Changing your title is nowhere near as stressful an experience as changing your given name, you'll need to notify organisations if you wish to change your title but you don't always need a deed poll or to go through a name-changing procedure, so marriage certificates changing your title from a Miss. to a Mrs. will be acceptable; as will a doctorate if you wish to change from Mr./Mrs./etc... to Dr.

If you are solely changing your surname to that of your spouse or civil partner, you do not need a deed poll, the marriage or civil partnership certificate will work just fine, and a lot of the steps in this book can be skipped. It will be known that this book will focus primarily on deed polls.

The big exception to this titular change rule is when you purchase a product that will "bestow a title upon you" or buy a product that will claim that you can become a Lord/Lady with an official title. These products that offer to give you a noble title are not illegal, but will not give you the title of Lord/Lady/Sir/etc... What is being purchased in most cases is in fact, a deed poll changing your name to Lord/Lady/Sir/etc... Joseph Bloggs with your new first name being Lord in this example; it is possible to have your driving licence under your new title that's officially a name. Expect many companies to consider you a joke, and some authorities may even reject your name change under this plan, as noble titles including those that are from the Order of the British Empire (MBE, OBE, etc...) can only be granted by the sovereign.

Before I continue with this, I should illustrate that changing your name doesn't need to be performed by a professional, and I am not qualified in the legal profession. The contents of this book highlight my experiences during my name-changing process, I will only state laws as they are at the time of writing if I know them, for more guidance and up-to-date information, you should consult the citizens' advice bureau, or a qualified family law solicitor or lawyer.

Step 1: Is a name change right for me?

A name change is designed for life, not just for a bet with your chums. You could easily declare a new name and not use it, reverse the name change the next day or tear up the deed poll altogether; it's like riding a bicycle blindfolded; you could do it, but this doesn't mean you should. If there's a family event that's caused you to experience anger or forced you to distance from your family members, I'd suggest talking to your family first to see if they'd approve or think you're making a sound decision; after all, the expectation is to make this name change permanent.

If your family are happy or if you're choosing to go through with it anyway, they may even try and suggest new names or try and influence your decision. My rule is if you consider changing your name for at least a few months beforehand and decide you still want to change, go for it.

Step 2: Choosing a Name

Since deciding that changing your name is something you're intending to do, you need to come up with an appropriate name or ultimately whatever you want to change it to; if you already know what your new identity will be, skip this but for those who aren't at all sure, stick around. But if you're only looking to change your surname, you could adopt the surname of another member of the family, a friend, an idol or a famous person, or if none of those ideas will work; go neutral and pick something common (Smith or Jones) or pick a name so obscure you could practically start your bloodline.

But when you're choosing a new name, you need to consider whether or not you'll actually respond (sounds daft, but if you've been known by one name for a long time, you'll instinctively answer your old name), your signature (we'll come to this soon), your new initials (don't call your new name: Sophia Helen Isabella Taylor without at least rearranging some of the middle names), and of course, be willing to stick to it.

Step 3: Legitimising a Document

You can have a deed poll one of two ways, 'enrolled' and 'unenrolled'; the only difference is that an enrolled deed poll is on public record at the Royal Courts of Justice, an unenrolled deed poll has just as much legal standing as an enrolled one and should be interpreted as a name change; however, one could argue that an enrolled deed poll is more likely to be performed in good faith as the document has been admitted via the courts. To change your name, you must be at least 16 to change your name via unenrolled deed poll; however, if you wish to enrol your deed poll, you can only do so at age eighteen and if you're a Commonwealth citizen. I ran into no obstacles with my unenrolled deed poll; in my situation, I was more than happy to save money by skipping enrolment of the deed poll with the Royal Courts of Justice. An enrolled deed poll costs £42.44 as of January 2023, whereas a standard/unenrolled deed poll can be as cheap as free.

Some companies will happily take some of your money for a document for a "legally valid" deed poll, these companies aren't providing anything special aside from a piece of parchment, and sometimes a fancy seal; some of these firms offer a "money back guarantee" in case something goes pear-shaped with the name change, but all of these deed polls are almost always unenrolled with the Royal Courts of Justice and carry the same weight as a home-made DIY deed poll.

If you're going through the DIY deed poll route, you need to state the following information:

"I (old name) of (your address) have given up my name (old name) and have adopted for all purposes the name (new name).

Signed as a deed on (date) as (old name) and (new name) in the presence of (witness 1 name) of (witness 1 address), and (witness 2 name) of (witness 2 address).

(new signature), (old signature)

(witness 1 signature), (witness 2 signature)."

The UK government website states that 2 witnesses are required for a deed poll to be legitimate; however, some deed poll documents also list the occupation of the witness. My deed poll only had one witness, a solicitor. My deed poll was accepted by the passport office, therefore I contacted the passport office to ask if they would require one or two witnesses on a document. Their answer was: in the case of an unenrolled DIY deed poll; 2 witnesses are necessary. Enrolled deed polls via the courts will make the name-changing process easier; if you have additional documentation, this should make the process easier, but it's not impossible.

I changed my name with a sole witness on an unenrolled deed poll back in 2018, the rules on pages from what I have researched have not changed since then, and anyone who is adding hurdles and hoops is most likely just covering their backs and 110% sure everything's compliant; even though from a legal standpoint, everything is lovely and legal. Having double the number of witnesses on the deed poll paper, (where one is fine) should be twice as nice.

Witnesses can be anyone as long as these criteria are fulfilled:

- They are not related to you, this includes partners, married or not.
- They don't live at the same address as you.

Work colleagues, neighbours, teachers, people on the street, and friends would be suitable witnesses. Some countries may require a document to be signed by a notary public or member of the legal profession for it to be legitimised, but check local laws before committing.

When the deed poll is signed, aside from a witness signature, you need to include your old signature as well as your new one. If you're changing your name by spelling or adding/removing a middle name, that may not necessarily be a challenge; if it's a new name entirely then you'll need to be a bit creative.

If you were born Jon Citizen and you had the above signature, that would be something fairly easy to sign, but imagine that you wanted to incorporate a middle name; your new signature would be different.

JRCitizen (signature)

Now, I am Jon Richard Citizen; the added initial is a significant enough change so banks & companies would be able to tell you are not the same person as Jon Citizen. But if you wanted to change name entirely, you would need some creativity.

JWWPerson (signature)

Jon William Wallace Person, is now a new name and by all definitions, a new signature; if your name is unimaginably long, has complicated middle names, or something that doesn't flow well on a pen; take a scrap of paper and try a few signatures, you could just write the name, write the initials, or sign your name but only your initials, your signature could be as simple as this:

In short, you need to come up with a new signature for everyday life as well as the original name change document, and you're not constrained as to what your signature can be. It'll only be unique to you.

Or if you skipped through this whole section, you could just write your name in full and call it an insignia; but as with changing the name, stick with it as if one signature is different, you could run into some challenges.

Step 4: Enforcing Your Name Change

Any new changes to your name will require any of these documents, as these are the most commonly accepted by companies and indeed by governmental organisations:

- Deed Poll
- Overseas or Domestic Marriage Certificate or Civil Partnership Certificate (can also be used for reverting to a birth name)
- Birth Certificate (only if reverting to your birth name, or adopted surname if using an adoption certificate)
- Decree nisi/absolute (only if reverting to your name prior to your divorce)

A comprehensive list of some of the authorities, and organisations you'll need to inform regarding your name change, think of this as a checklist once your name change has been carried out, and this list isn't in any particular order:

- Your employer (Difficulty: 1/5)

Approach your workplace HR department or your manager, with proof of the name change, and that's your first hurdle done; it's also worth updating your bank details with your employer as they may find it suspicious that your salary is paid into an account with your old name. I'll get onto updating bank details a little later.

- HMRC or Tax Office (Difficulty: 3/5)

This one involves writing a letter to the tax authority with a photocopy of your name change document and your current details to illustrate that you intend to change your name; you can also do this online or over the phone, where they may request proof of this change.

- Present School/College/University (Difficulty: 1/5)

When I changed my name at a young age, I felt smug with my stupidly long yet legitimate name on a piece of fancy paper and walked into my college's admin office to change my ID card with my new name. For most educational institutions, this is the process: walk in, state who you are, and present evidence that you go by a new name. If your college/university provides ID cards, they should print you a new one there and then. If you intend to change the name of a child under 16, this may involve going to the school with a copy of their birth certificate or new identification documents. It's a crucial reminder that deed polls are invalid if you're under 16.

- Exam Boards to Modify Certificates (Difficulty: 4/5)

If you want to change certificates of your academic and professional qualifications to those that show your new name, that can be possible; however, they will still be valid so long as you can prove your new name, by documentation. If you want to go the extra mile and get your certificates changed with your new name, the exam boards will charge a fee for the issue of new certificates. Pearson Qualifications for instance; will require 2 forms of ID and proof of the name change; the standard replacement certificate with UK delivery will cost £52 as of January 2023; however, the price and process ultimately depend on your exam board.

- NHS Records (Difficulty: 2/5)

This process is straightforward, this involved me walking into my GP with deed poll in hand, ID in the other, and the entire process was complete within less than 5 minutes; informing my GP of this change, this changed my details on the NHS register. If you have a private doctor, I'd do the same, walk in with your ID & proof of name change, and all should be changed in a matter of minutes.

- Dental Surgery (Difficulty: 2/5)

Unless your dentist is an NHS practice, you should still notify your dental clinic that you've changed your name. The best way is to send an e-mail with evidence attached or stroll into the dentist with your ID & proof that you've changed your name.

- HM Passport Office (Difficulty: 4/5)

For this change, you will need to apply for a new passport or perform a renewal of your current passport; even though I had six years left on my passport before it expired, I had to re-apply for a new document in the new name; presenting my old passport back to the passport office, I had to include the deed poll with the application and as I said in Step 3, my unenrolled deed poll worked fine. The cost for the renewal British adult passport in May 2023 is £82.50 if you apply online or £93 if you fill in a paper form.

- DVLA (Licence & Log Book) (Difficulty: 3/5)

Similar to the passport, you'll need to apply for a brand new driving licence if you're changing your name or gender using the D1 form; the big difference is that with a driving licence, it's free to change your name.

If you own a vehicle; fill in the sub-section of the log book that includes changing your name/address. Send evidence of the name change in case they request it. You may find that several organisations will only ask for proof if the name is substantially different (i.e. different first and surname).

- DVSA (if applicable) (Difficulty: 4/5)

This section is for those who have carried out additional driving qualifications; HGV drivers, driving instructors, taxi drivers, MOT testers, etc… Inform the DVSA that you go by a new name so that licences and certificates can be issued in your new identity; this may come at a cost, especially if your current certifications have not yet expired.

- Banks/Building Societies/Financial Institutions (Difficulty: 3/5)

Another place I found it a bit troublesome to change your name, the bank may decide to have its own rules regarding what they need to change your details, but ultimately they have to abide by

Data Protection (primarily the right to rectification, article 16 of the GDPR) and KYC (customer identification) laws. Annoyingly, it depends on your bank; but as a lenient example, it'll just involve presenting your bank card and evidence of the name change; your card may be cancelled while you wait for new cards bearing your new identity, so make sure you carry cash or have access to money during this time.

- Companies you hold shares (Difficulty: 3/5)

If you hold shares with a broker, you should take up your name change affairs with the broker, as they're responsible for keeping your correct personal information by law. If you're trading shares on an app, change your personal information on the app settings.

If you hold the shares with the individual companies, if a customer services or human resources department isn't available, you would need to take it up with either the director, treasurer, or any person with significant control of the company involved; this is because companies have a legal requirement to submit to Companies House who holds what shares in the company.

Ultimately, this depends on the nature of the companies involved; they could be lax or strict on their business compliance, and they may ask for proof of name change or new ID, or both, or they'll trust you.

- NS&I (Difficulty: 3/5)

If you're not familiar with NS&I, it's the state-owned organisation that's most well known for selling premium bonds as well as savings products; the difference between NS&I and the traditional banks is that they're bound to rules by the Financial Conduct Authority yet NS&I is also backed by the treasury; so expect to follow the same guidelines that you'd have to follow with your bank, the only downfall that NS&I has is that unlike a high street bank is that they are not accessible by branch so most likely, you'll submit your name change documentation digitally.

- Mortgage Provider (Difficulty: 2/5)

If your bank provides your mortgage, you shouldn't need to do much if this is the case; if the mortgage is done via your bank through another lender, broker, or a new company entirely, then you'll need to contact them with any possible account numbers you have. If another organisation holds the deed to the property when the mortgage is paid, the property will need to be issued with the correct name. You'll most likely go through some more hoops depending on who you're mortgaging with; This will be much easier than changing your name with the bank. If you don't have a mortgage because you've paid it off, contact the Land Registry.

- Landlord (Difficulty: 1/5)

Alternatively, if you don't own your home; simply inform your landlord. Your landlord should do this for free as the tenant is the same person in all but name; if your landlord is a housing association, council, or a corporate entity rather than an individual, you'll most likely need to send a copy via e-mail or the post with any account number you have so that the agreement can be amended with the new name.

- Utility Companies (Difficulty: 2/5)

Nobody wants someone else to be using their electricity, gas, water, etc… Make sure the companies know that you've changed your name by sending them a letter or e-mail with electronic proof of the name change, if they ask for me then they'll inform you, this should be free of charge.

- Council (Difficulty: 3/5)

This process is mainly relevant if you use council services, and if the council is your landlord, congratulations! You've eliminated 2 things off this list. This process of informing the authority may involve you either sending an e-mail or written communication so your council tax profile updates, if this won't work, then a visit to your local council building will need to be carried out. The process may be a long wait and this surely would be free of charge, with some chasing and prompt reminding then this process can be finalised faster than a pothole repair.

- Electoral Roll (Difficulty: 1/5)

Another easy process, I strolled into my local council building, specifically the arc that deals with Electoral Registration; I said what my old name was, and I changed it after I provided a copy of my new deed poll. When the next local election came around and my voting card arrived in the post, it listed my new name. Some councils might make the process a little complex by asking for identity documents, especially after the law recently changed requiring ID at polling stations.

- Mobile Phone Provider (Difficulty: 2/5)

With most bills, if you need to keep a service running, you should inform whoever provides your mobile phone service that you've changed your name; this is especially if you have a handset on a contract or if you've signed up for online services. If there's a stipulation in your contract that there's a fee to change your details, there may not be much you can do.

- TV Licensing (Difficulty: 2/5)

The bill of which you receive your licence and if you have a payment card, both need to be updated; this should involve sending a copy of your name change and a note with your current information, and their records should update pretty quickly.

- Credit Provider (Difficulty: 3/5)

In a similar system when you change your details with the bank, you'll most likely need to provide electronic or physical evidence of the name change, you'll automatically get a new card in your new name if it's a credit card you're changing, rendering your old credit cards obsolete. Loans may come with a clause that state you may need to pay a fee as these are for a fixed term, but when this is updated, it will in turn update your credit file.

- Pension Provider (Difficulty: 4/5)

Often forgotten, if you've left a previous employer who contributed to a workplace pension in your old name, inform the pension company of your change. There could be difficulties if a name change isn't evidenced or isn't otherwise changed, so give them a phone call or e-mail and inform the provider of your situation. If they can change the name on your behalf, then you need to upload the name change document. Pension companies are tightly regulated, so you may need more information to back up your name change.

I used to work in a financial planning firm dealing with many pensions from different providers, if you've worked for multiple employers, you'll be bamboozled by how many workplace pensions you never knew you had.

- Insurance Companies (Difficulty: 3/5)

Whether it's for your car, house, travel plans, medical, etc... You need to inform your insurer that you've changed your name; as at best, it'll slightly complicate the claims process or worse, invalidate your claim. Car insurance companies are notorious for adding clauses that charge you for changing details (i.e. address, car make and model, occupation, among other things). So if you're willing to wait until after your policy expires to change your name, you would save some money on the admin fees; you risk invalidating your policies, so change it at the same time if possible.

Insurers may not even ask for evidence but if your insurance company has an online portal, upload the name change document online or post a copy if they ask for it. If you have breakdown coverage with your insurance, the insurer should update this on your behalf; if it's with another company, let them know too. Breakdown cover organisations sometimes charge a fee to change your details.

- Mail-Order Companies (Difficulty: 1/5)

For the few of you who still order stuff by mail catalogues, let them know as if you end up buying anything, they'll send it to the right person; this could also be extended to those who use a milkman/woman for groceries.

- Professional bodies (Difficulty: 2/5)

Whether it's a firm that manages qualifications or professional memberships, let them know so you can get all your information right. These bodies are under strict regulation in some cases so send them a paper copy of your documents if possible.

- Clubs, societies, and associations (Difficulty: 1/5)

If these are clubs such as the Citroen C3 owners club or a model railway preservation charity, you'll find that verbal proof may be enough but showing an electronic copy of your name change to the treasurer or president of your group should suffice.

- Transport authorities (Difficulty: 2/5)

This one only truly applies if you're a user of public transport; we're talking about bus passes, rail cards, and even bike hire where you might hold membership. You could be in a lot of trouble if you're travelling under a different person's travel pass just because you didn't change the name on the card.

- Internet Service Provider (Difficulty: 2/5)

For another organisation that involves contractual change, your broadband company should do this for free but may charge an admin fee. Just send them an e-mail or phone them regarding the change and send them evidence if requested.

- Student Loans Company (Difficulty: 3/5)

Nobody likes paying their student loans, but as repaying student debt is linked with your earnings, whether you're employed in a company or self-employed; let the Student Loans Company know that you've changed your name so they know you're still paying your student loan. The SLC reserve the right to take legal action over unpaid student debts, as with most debt agreements.

- Social Media Websites (Difficulty: 1/5)

For many social media platforms, changing your name is as easy as changing a text box, however for some, it isn't. Websites reserve the right to ask for proof of this new identity, whether it's a driving licence or passport in the new identity or a simple document to verify the change.

- E-mail (Difficulty: 5/5)

This process won't be a concern if your e-mail is 'electricpants@email.com' or an address that doesn't contain what will be your 'old' identity, but of course, having an old name in the address for the receiving point of all your electronic communication may be a concern, most definitely if you're changing your identity because you're a victim of stalking, harassment, or in any form of danger. Getting a new e-mail address is straightforward, but you will need to change your e-mail on every website that you regularly use; if that's not allowed, then you will need to contact the technical support sector of that website, and should this tactic fail; you will need to re-register.

Words cannot express how difficult I found this part, especially if you need to be sure you've got a new e-mail address on file for every website you wish to maintain an account. I fell into the trap of deactivating my old e-mail address too soon; because of that, I couldn't log in to my e-mail and easily reset my password and therefore had to start new accounts for websites from scratch.

- Law Enforcement (Difficulty: 4/5)

If you have ever been convicted, cautioned, prosecuted, arrested, or had any negative run-ins with the law that resulted in a criminal record, you are obliged to notify the police station about your name change as soon as possible; this is also applicable for people who are on probation or released under licence or bail conditions. You cannot change your name and not notify your probation officer. Just because you were a criminal, it does not deprive you of the right to change your name; this also includes those on the sex offenders register; you also have the right to change your name, however, you must inform the police within three days; required in the Sexual Offences Act of 2003.

Another good strategy once you've informed all of the above, is to live your life for the next 12 months; and if there's any mail that arrives at your property in your old name, politely inform them that you now go by another name and you're known as such; unless if it's junk mail, send it back to them in the same envelope, write "return to sender, unsolicited mail" after that, they should leave you alone as the companies have to pay to receive the unsolicited mail back.

Changing Your Name in Scotland

The rules and advice for changing your name in Scotland remain mostly the same but there are limits that Scotland-born citizens and residents face and additional routes if they wish to take them but the process and ease of the name change remain mostly the same.

It's not necessary but it's advised to have the name change recorded with the Registrar General; in some cases, it would not be advised to have the change recorded; for example, in the case of domestic violence or stalking. A change of name is recorded on a public register and anyone would have access to the change of name.

The Scottish Registrar General is only available to you if you were born or adopted in Scotland; if not, you can use the standard deed poll method. It's a good idea that if you want to show that you have changed your name more formally, you can choose to enrol your deed poll at the Royal Courts of Justice. The Registrar General in Scotland however does impose a limit on the number of times you can change your name:

- For a child under the age of two, only one change of first name can be recorded.

- Only one change of first name and middle name can be recorded for children aged between two and sixteen.

- For people over the age of sixteen, only one change of first name and up to three changes of surname may be recorded; and after a change of surname has been recorded, a period of five years must pass before another change is made.

Bear in mind, a name change can still be made if these limits have been exceeded, but these changes just cannot be registered with the Registrar General.

If you don't wish to record your name change with the Registrar General, you can still change your name with a standard deed poll or a statutory declaration. It is much easier to change your name with a statutory declaration than it is going through the registrar or courts, and this statutory declaration is not a deed poll but they're almost the same. A deed poll is less wordy and requires witnesses for the change to be valid; a statutory declaration on the other hand doesn't need any witnesses but does need to be overseen by a professional who can administer oaths (i.e. a solicitor, court officer, or notary public).

Changing Your Name in Northern Ireland

The process for changing your name in Northern Ireland is a little different but still simple if you want to use a short route; a standard deed poll works here in the same way as a deed poll would work in England, Wales, or Scotland if you're sixteen years old; but if you're under 18 and you wish to have your name changed, there is an application that your parents can fill in, where someone with significant control can sign a document to change your name until you turn eighteen.

If you're eighteen or older, you can also apply to legally change your name with the General Register Office of Northern Ireland if you want an alternative route; bear in mind with this method; there are some set rules, by the General Register Office that are similar to the regulations in Scotland:

- For a child under the age of eighteen, only one change of first names or surname can be recorded.
- For people over the age of eighteen, only one change of first name and up to three changes of surname may be recorded;

and after a change of surname has been recorded, a period of five years must pass before another change is made.

The fee set by the General Register Office of Northern Ireland is £35 whether it's for an adult or child.

When changing your name with the General Register Office, you'll need to have your application signed by a lay magistrate or a Justice of the Peace, they will not charge to sign your name change documentation.

If you want to skip the route of the General Register Office, you can still opt for an unenrolled deed poll and the standard rules still apply.

Information for Foreign Citizens

A Marriage certificate or decree nisi/absolute should be acceptable proof that you have relinquished an old name. In the UK, if you change your name by deed poll, your nationality and citizenship won't stop you from performing an unenrolled deed poll; the challenge starts when your country of origin may not accept the name change, speak with your consulate or embassy before you go ahead with the name change as there may be more information required. If you are a foreign citizen residing in the UK, UK laws apply, therefore a deed poll made in the UK will still be valid; however, if you wish to enrol your deed poll with the Royal Courts of Justice, you can only do so if you're a citizen of a Commonwealth country, or if you're a Commonwealth citizen as defined under the British Nationality Act of 1981. According to a Royal Courts of Justice document published in 2021, you must be a citizen of any of these countries to enrol your deed poll with the Royal Courts of Justice: **Antigua & Barbuda, Australia, The Bahamas, Bangladesh, Barbados, Belize, Botswana, Brunei, Canada, Cyprus, Dominica, Eswatini, Fiji, The Gambia, Ghana, Grenada, Guyana, India, Jamaica, Kenya, Kiribati, Lesotho, Malawi, Malaysia, Maldives, Malta, Mauritius, Namibia, Nauru, New Zealand, Nigeria, Pakistan, Papua New Guinea, St. Kitts &**

Nevis, St. Lucia, St. Vincent & the Grenadines, Samoa, Seychelles, Sierra Leone, Singapore, Solomon Islands, South Africa, Sri Lanka, Tanzania, Tongo, Trinidad & Tobago, Tuvalu, Uganda, Vanuatu, Zambia, and Zimbabwe.

If you're not a citizen of the countries above, you cannot enrol your deed poll with the courts but an unenrolled deed poll will still be valid. If you're also a foreign national, you should also inform your home country's embassy so they can issue a new passport in your new identity, and you should also inform the home office and immigration service that you've changed your name; this is so that your visa can be updated, you will most likely need to pay for these services.

Closing Remarks

I was given 'advice' from people even by those who still think that you should keep the name you've always had and never deviate, that this book was unnecessary; I disagree with that for a myriad of reasons.

My rationale for writing this book was that there weren't many books on how to change your name in the UK, you could find a lot if you were in some U.S. states for example but even though the principle remains the same, keeping to the law by the letter would always be different across the pond. The minority of books that were published and available from the British Library were older than I am, so I felt it was necessary to give a fresh approach with up-to-date regulations, especially since when I was born, Scotland and Northern Ireland had devolved parliaments and like to shake things up compared to the rest of the nation.

I also wanted to give my account and experience so that if you're trying to distance yourself from former family or you've felt like you want to take a new path in your life, you're not alone and the process of waking up and adopting a new persona and identity has fascinated my younger self for such a long time, finally having the guts to do it was a load off my shoulders and felt like I had a lot more free will.

I laugh in the face of people who say you ruin the family with your decision to change your name and jeopardise the bloodline, a true family will stick by you, and people change their identities all the time; look at married couples and adopted children. This journey can be re-journeyed by anyone and in my eyes, it was worth it whatever you decide to do with your new identity, seize it, be proud of who you want to become, and I wish you all the best in the future.

www.ingramcontent.com/pod-product-compliance
Lightning Source LLC
Chambersburg PA
CBHW080212040426
42333CB00043B/2625